CAMBRIDGE
Global English

Learner's Book

1

Caroline Linse and Elly Schottman

CAMBRIDGE
UNIVERSITY PRESS

CAMBRIDGE
UNIVERSITY PRESS

University Printing House, Cambridge CB2 8BS, United Kingdom

One Liberty Plaza, 20th Floor, New York, NY 10006, USA

477 Williamstown Road, Port Melbourne, VIC 3207, Australia

4843/24, 2nd Floor, Ansari Road, Daryaganj, Delhi – 110002, India

79 Anson Road, #06–04/06, Singapore 079906

Cambridge University Press is part of the University of Cambridge.

It furthers the University's mission by disseminating knowledge in the pursuit of education, learning and research at the highest international levels of excellence.

www.cambridge.org
Information on this title: www.cambridge.org/9781107676091

© Cambridge University Press 2014

First published 2014
20 19 18 17 16 15

Printed in Dubai by Oriental Press

A catalogue record for this publication is available from the British Library

ISBN 978-1-107-67609-1 Learner's Book with Audio CDs (2)

Cambridge University Press has no responsibility for the persistence or accuracy of URLs for external or third-party internet websites referred to in this publication, and does not guarantee that any content on such websites is, or will remain, accurate or appropriate.

Welcome to Cambridge Global English Stage 1

Cambridge Global English is an eight-stage course for learners of English as a Second Language (ESL). The eight stages range from the beginning of primary (Stages 1–6) to the end of the first two years of junior secondary (Stages 7–8). It is ideal for all international ESL learners, and particularly for those following the Cambridge Primary/Secondary English as a Second Language Curriculum Framework, as it has been written to adhere to this framework. It also presents realistic listening and reading texts, writing tasks, and end-of-unit projects similar to those students might encounter in the context of a first-language school. These elements provide teachers with the opportunity to tailor the level of challenge to meet the needs of their particular students. The course is organised into nine thematic units of study which include a range of activities, text types and objectives.

Cambridge Global English materials are aligned with the Common European Framework of Reference. The materials reflect the following principles:

- *An international focus*. Specifically developed for young learners throughout the world, the topics and situations in *Cambridge Global English* have been selected to reflect this diversity and encourage learning about each other's lives through the medium of English.
- *An enquiry-based, language-rich approach to learning*. *Cambridge Global English* engages children as active, creative learners. At the same time as participating in a range of curriculum-based activities, they can acquire content knowledge, develop critical thinking skills and practise English language and literacy.

- *English for educational success*. To meet the challenges of the future, learners will need to develop facility with both conversational and more formal English. From the earliest stage, *Cambridge Global English* addresses both these competencies. Emphasis is placed on developing the listening, speaking, reading and writing skills learners will need to be successful in using English-language classroom materials.

In addition to this Learner's Book, *Cambridge Global English Activity Book 1* provides supplementary support and practice. Comprehensive support for teachers is available in *Cambridge Global English Teacher's Resource 1*.

The following icons are used in this Learner's Book:

- 🔊 pre-recorded listening activity
- 🎵 pre-recorded song and class singing activity
- 💬 pairwork or small group speaking activity (not mediated by teacher)
- 📝 write in notebook activity
- [AB] linking activity in Activity Book
- [1+2] cross-curricular maths activity
- 🔬 cross-curricular science activity.

We hope that learners and teachers enjoy using *Cambridge Global English Stage 1* as much as we have enjoyed writing it.

Caroline Linse and Elly Schottman

Contents

4

Listening/Speaking	School subjects	Phonics / Word study	Critical thinking / Values
Listen to letters, numbers and colours	Maths: Number review	Alphabet review	

Listen for information
Listen to letters
Interviews
Discuss, act out poems and songs
	Geography	Letter names
		Spelling
		Capital letters
		Labels
			Understanding and conducting
			  interviews
			Organising and making charts
			Making friends, working, playing
			  and learning together

Listen for information
Ask and answer
Talk about families
Discuss, act out poems and songs
	Maths: 1–10, simple problem
	  solving
	Geography
	Social studies
		th
		Short *a*
		Rhyming words
			Families in different parts of the world
			Asking survey questions, creating and
			  discussing graphs
			Classification
			How families work and play together

Listen to / give instructions
Make a new song verse
Discuss and act out poems, songs,
  stories
	Physical education	Short *u*
		Rhyming words
		Question marks
		Read and act out
		  decodable story
			What games can we play?
			Creative problem solving
			Compare and contrast
			Taking turns, speaking politely,
			  being a good sport

Listen for information
Ask and talk about pictures
Discuss and act out poems, songs,
  stories
	Arts and crafts
	Shapes and colours
	Make puppets
		Short *e*
		I'm (contractions)
		Rhyming words
			What can we make with colours
			  and shapes?
			Recognising and reproducing
			  word patterns
			Planning and making a quilt
			Helping others
			Cleaning up after ourselves

Interviews
Guided speaking
Discuss and act out stories, poems,
  songs
Sing new verses
Ask and answer information questions
	Science: Life cycles
	Growing vegetables
		Short *i*, *ch*, *sh*
		Tongue twisters
		Identify rhyming words
		I'm/we're (contractions)
			What can you find on a farm?
			Document growth of seeds
			Interpreting diagrams
			Story maps
			Taking care of plants and animals
			  is important

Talk about ability Talk about senses Act out a story	Music Science: Senses Arts and crafts: Making instruments	Short *o* *-er* forms Compare minimal pairs Rhyming sounds	How do we use our five senses? Making lists Comparing things Understanding high and low sounds Inclusion/awareness of disability Respecting differences

Listen for information
Talk about transportation
  and movement
Listen to stories, poems
Song
	Arts and crafts: Making a
	  helicopter
	Science: Hands-on
	  exploration, shapes
		Long *e* sound
		Listen for sounds
			How do we travel around?
			Classifying and identifying difference
			  between vehicles and movement
			Keeping safe while using
			  transportation

Listening comprehension Guided speaking Dialogues Emphatic expression Discuss and act out stories, poems, songs	Science and the environment Weather patterns Experiment: Things that float	Long *a* spellings *ai* and *ay* Punctuation and capitals	Why is water important? Providing examples to support ideas Predicting outcomes Understanding nature and survival Understanding the importance of water
Listening comprehension: Routes Talk about where you live Act out conversation Play games Perform poems Ask for and give things	Social studies: Living in cities	*-y* endings Awareness of syllables Rhyming words	What can you see, hear and do in a city? Interpreting maps Interpreting poems We can appreciate where we live We can respect different opinions

Aa

apple

Bb

book

Cc

cat

Dd

duck

Ii

insect

Jj

jacket

Kk

kite

Ll

leaf

Qq

quilt

Rr

rain

Ss

sun

Tt

table

Yy
yellow

Zz

zoo

Ee

egg

Ff

fish

Gg

guitar

Hh

hand

Mm

mouth

Nn
q
nine

Oo

octopus

Pp

pencil

Uu

umbrella

Vv

violin

Ww

window

Xx
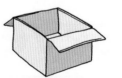
box

one	1	
two	2	
three	3	
four	4	
five	5	
six	6	
seven	7	
eight	8	
nine	9	
ten	10	

Colours

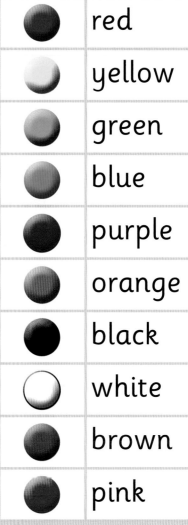

●	red
●	yellow
●	green
●	blue
●	purple
●	orange
●	black
○	white
●	brown
●	pink

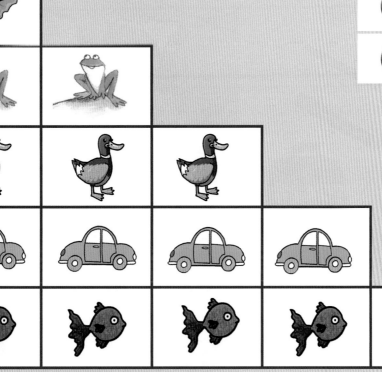

1 Welcome to school

1 Think about it — What do we do at school?

③ 1 Read and listen

Find each thing in the picture.

> **Hello, school!**
> Tables and chairs
> A list of rules
> Books and crayons
> Hello, school!

2 What's in the classroom?

Find some more things.

a blue pencil

a green ruler

a red lunchbox

④ 3 💬 Making friends

Listen to the children talking.
How old are they?
Practise with your partner.

4 Topic vocabulary

Listen, point and say.

a table

a clock

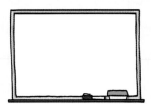

a whiteboard

an ABC chart

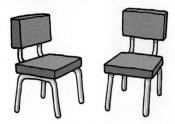

chairs

computers

6 5 Classroom treasure hunt

Listen to Matteo. He is doing a classroom treasure hunt.

Which thing does he forget to say?

Now do a treasure hunt in your classroom!

6 School poem

Write a school poem with your class.

2 Find out more Children around the world

7 **1 Before you read**

Look at these photos.
What do the children do at school?
Now listen and read.

1 Amira from Oman

My name is Amira. I am 6.
I use computers at school.

2 Marat from Kazakhstan

My name is Marat. I am 7.
I read at school.

3 Zak from New Zealand

My name is Zak. I am 6.
I do Maths at school.

Writing tip

A name begins with a
capital letter. **Amira**, **Marat**, **Zak**

2 **What do you do at school?**

Write about yourself. Draw a picture.

read

use computers

write

do Maths

sing

draw

My name is ___ .
I am ___ .
I ___ at school.

3 How do children go to school?

Read and listen.

I go by bicycle.

We go by bus.

I go by car.

We go by boat.

We walk.

4 AB 1+2 A class chart

How do **you** go to school? Make a chart with your class.

How do you go to school?					
I go by bus.	Lara	Aron	Tanya	Ali	Paco
I go by car.	Kuldip	Marta	Sara		
I go by bicycle.	Lucas				
I walk.	Pablo	Dina			

3 Letters and sounds

🎵 1 Alphabet poem

Listen and point to the letters.

PHOTOCOPY ONLY
DO NOT CUT
OR WRITE IN BOOK

A B C D E F G
We're in school, you and me.

H I J K L M N
I have a pencil. You have a pen.

O P Q R S T
Look around. What do you see?

U V W X Y Z
Put your hands on your head!

2 Word wall

Make a word wall with your class.
What's the first letter of your name? Put your name under that letter.

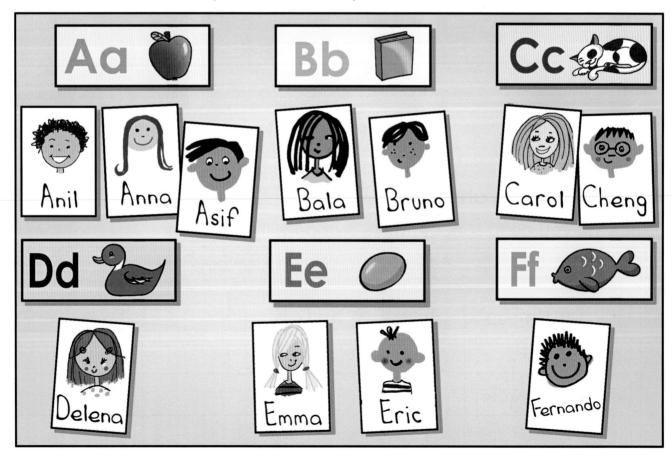

3 🎵 **A spelling song**

Make 5 letter cards.
Point to the letters as you sing.

Bingo

There was a farmer had a dog
And Bingo was its name-o.
B-I-N-G-O!   B-I-N-G-O! B-I-N-G-O!
And Bingo was its name-o!

4 📝 🎵 **Make a new song**

Sing some new verses! Make letter cards. Point to the letters as you sing.

R E A D

Every day we read at school,
We read with our teacher.
R-E-A-D.   R-E-A-D.   R-E-A-D.
We read with our teacher.

S I N G

Every day we sing at school,
We sing with our teacher.
S-I-N-G.   S-I-N-G.   S-I-N-G.
We sing with our teacher.

4 Use of English — Favourite colours

11 1 Colours

Listen and point to the colours.
Can you think of something
for each colour?

red	**orange**
blue	**black**
green	**purple**
yellow	**pink**
brown	**white**

a **red** apple

a **blue** pencil

12 2 An interview

Listen to Fatima.
She is interviewing Ben.
What questions does
she ask?

Name: Ben

Favourite colour: black

Fatima interviews
another friend.
What is her name?
What is her favourite
colour?

Name: ___

Favourite colour: ___

3 📝 AB Make a name card

Draw a picture of yourself. Write your name and your favourite colour.

4 **Interview a friend**

Ask your partner some questions.

What's your name?

Can you spell your name, please?

What's your favourite colour?

Write about your partner. Then introduce your partner to the class.

This is my friend.
His name is ___ .
His favourite colour is ___ .

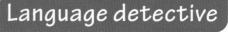
Language detective

When do we say **his** and **her**?

This is my friend.
Her name is ___ .
Her favourite colour is ___ .

This is a girl.
Her name begins with R.
Her favourite colour is red.

5 **Mystery child**

Choose a name card.
Tell your partner about the child.
Can they guess who it is?

 Name: Anna
Favourite colour: yellow

 Name: Rosa
Favourite colour: red

 Name: Tomas
Favourite colour: green

 Name: Lan
Favourite colour: orange

5 Read and respond

1 Before you read

This poem tells a story about a girl. The girl is going to school.
Look at the pictures. What do you think happens?
Now listen and read.

I go to school

by Richard Brown and Kate Ruttle

I go to school in the morning and I look like this.

I see a little rabbit and it hops like this.

I see a little duck and it swims like this.

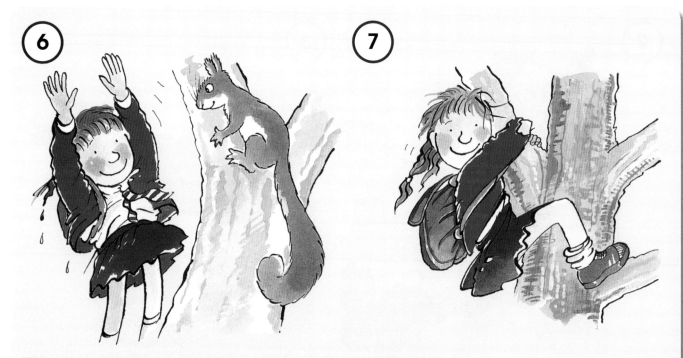

I see a little squirrel and it climbs like this.

Words to remember

Find this word in the story. How many times can you see it?

I

I go to school in the morning and I look like this!

2 Yes or no

Does the girl see these things on her way to school? Say **yes** or **no**.

 a duck

 a bus

 a rabbit

 a squirrel

3 🗨 Over to you

What do you see on your way to school?

 I see cars.

 cars

 ducks

 bicycles

 children

4 🗨 What do the animals do?

Match the pictures.
Say the sentences.

1 A squirrel

swims.

2 A rabbit

climbs.

3 A duck

hops.

6 Choose a project   What do we do at school?

A Make word cards

Write a word then draw a picture. What letter does the word start with?
Add the word cards to the word wall.

car

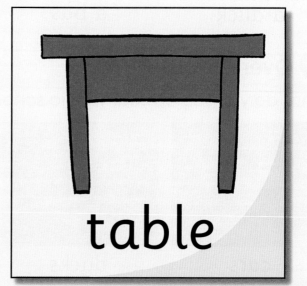

table

B Write a poem

Read this poem.
Then write a poem with your friends.
What do you do at school?

School

We **read** at school

We **write** at school

We **draw** at school

School is cool!

C Make a colour book

Choose a colour – for example, red.
Take photos or draw pictures of things that are red.

a red pencil a red book

Write words under each picture.

L👀k what I can do!

- I can say the names of things in my classroom.

- I can say what I do at school.

- I can write my name.

- I can read and write the letters of the alphabet. **Aa Bb Cc Dd Ee**

- I can introduce a friend.

23

1 Think about it   What do families do together?

14 1 Read and listen

Is your family big or small?

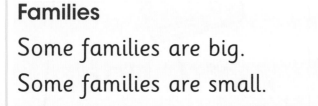

Families

Some families are big.
Some families are small.
I love my family best of all.

15 2 Sam and his family

Sam is talking about his family. What do they do every Saturday evening?

Listen, point and say.

Then listen to Sam talking about his family. Is it true? Say **yes** or **no.**

mother mum

father dad

brother

sister

Which words have a **th** sound in the middle?

Which two words rhyme?

Which words mean the same?

grandpa

grandma

4 Do you … ?

Ask and answer questions about your family.

Do you read books with your family?

Yes, I do.

No, I don't.

read books

watch TV

fly kites

play games

5 Make a card!

Make a card for someone in your family. Write a message.

Dear Dad,
This card is for you.
Love,
Lily

17 **1 Before you read**

Look at the pictures. What do the children eat for breakfast?
Now listen and read.

John lives in the United States.
He eats pancakes for breakfast.

Trang lives in Vietnam.
She eats noodles for breakfast.

2 **What do you eat for breakfast?**

Ask your partner.

> What do you eat for breakfast?

> I eat cereal with milk.

bread

rice

beans

eggs

soup

yogurt

noodles

cereal with milk

fruit

3 **Write**

Write about yourself and your partner.

What do you eat for breakfast?

I eat ___ .

What does your partner eat for breakfast?

___ eats ___ .

4 Talia and Jacob's fruit salad

Read and listen to the recipe.
Point to the correct pictures
as you read.

My sister and I eat
fruit salad for breakfast.
This is our recipe.

apple

banana

grapes

1 mango
10 grapes
1 banana
4 strawberries

• Wash the fruit.
• Cut up the fruit.
• Eat your fruit salad.

mango

strawberry

pineapple

5 Write a recipe

Make your own fruit salad recipe. Which fruits do you like?

6 A class chart

Look at the chart. How many children like bananas?
How many children don't like bananas?

watermelon

orange

Do you like bananas?								
Yes, I do.	●	●	●	●	●	●	●	
No, I don't.	●	●	●					

Make your own class chart.

pear

3 Letters and sounds — Short a

apple **cat**

19 **1 Listen and look**

Listen to the short **a** sound. Say the words.

20 **2 Grandma's glasses**

Listen to the rhyme. Say it.

Here are Gr**a**ndma's glasses.
Here is Gr**a**ndma's h**a**t.
This is how she folds her h**a**nds
And puts them on her l**a**p.

3 Rhyming words

Say the words.
How are they the same?
How are they different?

map   lap   nap

Here are two other words that rhyme with **map**.
Spell and say these words.

c ＿ ＿   c l ＿ ＿

4 Phonics story

Read and listen.

The cat

The cat has a hat.

The cat has a map.

The cat claps.

The cat is back.

The cat has a nap in Dad's lap.

Listen again. How many words do you hear with the short **a** sound?

4 Use of English Let's count!

1 [1+2] **How many?**

How many doors are there?

There is 1 door.

How many windows are there?

There are 4 windows.

How many doors and windows are there in your house?

2 💬 **Play a counting game**

Use a pencil and paper clip. Spin the paper clip.
Ask and answer questions. Take turns.

How many beds are there?

There are 2 beds.

3 📝 🔢 🎵 **Sing a counting song**

Make number cards.

Count and point from 1 to 10. Then count backwards from 10 to 1.

1 2 3 4 5 6 7 8 9 10

Listen to the song. Point to the number cards.
Sing the song.

Ten in the bed

There are **10** in the bed
And the little one says,
'Roll over. Roll over.'
So they all roll over and 1 falls out.

There are **9** in the bed
And the little one says,
'Roll over. Roll over.'
So they all roll over and 1 falls out.

. . . .

There is **1** in the bed
And the little one says, 'Good night!'

Roll over!

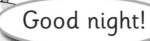

Good night!

5 Read and respond

23 **1 Before you read**

Look at the photos. What do you think this text is about?

Now listen and read.

Families work and have fun

In a family there are grown-ups and children.

This family is small.

This family is big.

The grown-ups work.

This mum cooks the dinner.

This dad works on the computer.

The children work.

This boy lays the table.

This girl tidies her room.

Families have fun together.

These children play together.

These men talk and laugh together.

People in a family help each other.

9

This boy helps his little sister.
'Thank you,' says the girl.

10

This girl helps her little brother.
'Thank you,' says the boy.

2 💬 Family questionnaire

Ask the questions and read the answers with your partner.

Big and small families

How many grown-ups are there in your family?

How many children are there in your family?

Work

Do you lay the table?	yes	no	sometimes
Do you tidy your room?	yes	no	sometimes
Do you do homework?	yes	no	sometimes

Fun

Do you play games?	yes	no	sometimes
Do you watch TV?	yes	no	sometimes
Do you talk and laugh?	yes	no	sometimes

3 📝 AB Draw and write

How do you help your family? Draw a picture.

Write a sentence about your picture.

Writing tip

A sentence begins with a capital letter.

Most sentences end with a full stop.

He helps his dad.

Words to remember

Find these words in the text:

this   his   her.

A Make a chart

Think of a question.

Do you like … ?

Do you like eggs?

Yes, I do.

Ask 10 people. Mark the answers on a chart.

Do you like … ?									
Yes, I do.									
No, I don't.									

B Learn a poem

Act out the words or draw pictures.
Teach the poem to your class.

Good morning, Mother Hen

Chook, chook, chook, chook, chook.

Good morning, Mother Hen.

How many chicks have you got?

Oh my, I have 10.

4 of them are yellow.

4 of them are brown.

And 2 of them are speckled red,

The nicest in the town.

c Make a counting book

Take photos or draw pictures. Write words under each picture.

1 car   2 cats

LOOk what I can do!

- I can talk about families.

- I can read and write numbers up to 10.

 1 2 3 4 5  6 7 8  9 10

- I can ask and answer questions about food:
  Do you like ... ?

- I can read and write words with the short **a** sound.

cat

3 Fun and games

1 Think about it   What games can we play?

24 1 Read and listen

Clap the rhythm.
Try bouncing a ball as you read!

> **Bounce the ball**
> Ball, ball,
> Bounce the ball!
> Roll it, throw it,
> Catch the ball!

25 2 Which picture?

Listen. Point to the right picture.

Listen, point and say.
Then listen again and do the action.

throw   catch   roll

hit   kick   bounce

Listen to the letters. What word do they spell? Say the word.

4 Can you do it?

Find out which things you and your partner can do.
Go and try! Then tell the class.

- Bounce a ball 4 times.

- Roll a ball to your partner.

- Catch a small ball.

- Hit a ball with a bat.

- Catch a big ball.

- Throw a ball into a box.

Can you catch a big ball?

Yes, I can.

5 Make up a game with a ball

You can use a ball, a box and other things. Write and draw pictures.

27 **1** 💬 **Read and play**

Read and listen to the instructions.
Play the game.

Rock, paper, scissors

How to play:

You need 2 people.

1 Face your partner.

2 Say: 1, 2, 3, Go!

3 Make one of these signs with your hand.

4 Look at your partner's hand and your hand.

Who wins the game?

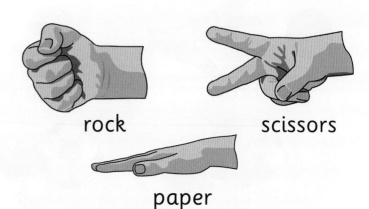

rock   scissors

paper

paper   rock   Paper can cover a rock, so **paper** wins.

rock   scissors   A rock can break scissors, so **rock** wins.

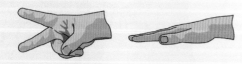   

scissors   paper   Scissors can cut paper, so **scissors** win.

Play **Rock, paper, scissors** with a partner. Who wins?
Play the game 5 times.

2 💬 **Read, play and compare**

Here is a game from Malaysia. Play this game too.

Bird, water, rock

How to play:

You need 2 people.

1 Face your partner.

2 Say: 1, 2, 3, Go!

3 Make one of these signs with your hand.

4 Look at your partner's hand and your hand. Who wins the game?

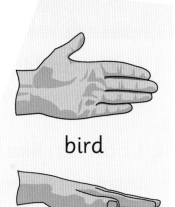

bird

water

rock

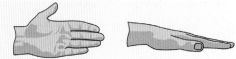 

bird   water    A bird can drink water, so **bird** wins.

water   rock    Water can cover a rock, so ___ .

rock   bird   A rock can hit a bird, so ___ .

Play **Bird, water, rock** with a partner. Who wins? Play the game 5 times.

3 [AB] Similar or different?

How are these two games similar? How are they different?

3 Letters and sounds   Short u

cup   bug

29 **1 Listen and look**

Listen to the short **u** sound. Say the words.

29 **2 I can run like a puppy**

Listen to the poem. Say it.

I can r**u**n like a p**u**ppy.

I can j**u**mp like a b**u**g.

I can b**u**zz like a bee.

I can sit on the r**u**g.

3 💬 **Rhyming game 'Tic-tac-toe'**

Each player makes 9 counters. Write a word from this list on each counter:

bug   truck   sun   flag   hat   cut   sad   cup   clap.

Choose a picture. Say the word. Find a counter with a
rhyming word and put it on the picture. Take turns with
your partner. To win, put 3 counters in a row.

Counter examples:

cat	up	duck
rug	dad	bag
run	map	nut

bug   truck

bug   truck

30 4 Phonics story

Read and listen.

Listen again. How many words do you hear with the short **u** sound?

Run, duck, run!

This duck runs.

The duck is in the mud.
She's stuck!

The duck goes up.

The muddy duck
runs again.

5 Puppets

Make puppets for the duck, the truck and the puddle.
Act out the story.

4 Use of English Giving instructions

1 Where is the duck?

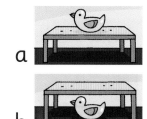

a

1 The duck is **on** the table.

2 The duck is **under** the table.

b

3 The duck is **next to** the table.

c

2 💬 Play an instructions game

Play this game with some friends. One player gives an instruction.
The other players follow the instructions.

Put your	pencil	on	your ____
	finger	**next to**	
	hand	**under**	

Put your pencil under your nose.

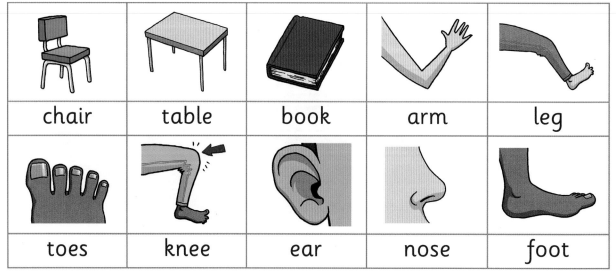

| chair | table | book | arm | leg |
| toes | knee | ear | nose | foot |

31 **3 Left and right**

Match the pictures and the instructions.

1 Put your right hand on the table.

2 Touch your right ear.

3 Shake your left foot.

Listen to and follow the instructions.

a

b

c

32 **4 Point to the baby**

Listen to the instructions. Point with your finger.

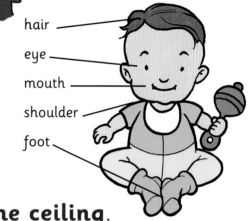

hair
eye
mouth
shoulder
foot

33 **5** 🎵 **Wind the bobbin up**

Follow the instructions. Sing and dance!

Chorus:

Wind the bobbin up.

Wind the bobbin up.

Pull, pull. Clap, clap, clap.

Point to **your shoulders**.

Point to **your nose**.

Point to **your ears** and

Point to **your toes**.

Clap your hands together, 1, 2, 3.

Put your hands upon your knees.

Chorus

Point to **the ceiling**.

Point to **the floor**.

Point to **the window** and

Point to **the door**.

Clap your hands together, 1, 2, 3.

Put your hands upon your knees.

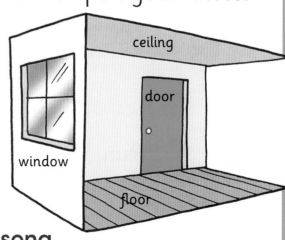

ceiling
door
window
floor

6 💬 🄰🄱 🎵 **Make up a new verse of the song**

Teach your new verse to a partner or your class.

5 Read and respond

34 1 Before you read

This is a play about animals. The small pictures show
which animal is speaking. Listen and read. Find the pictures
of **a rabbit**, **2 ducks**, **3 frogs**, and **a lion**.

The Ker-PLUNK

A rabbit is having a nap by a pond.
The rabbit hears a strange and scary sound.
Ker-PLUNK!

 Help! A scary Ker-PLUNK! Run, run, run!

 What's wrong, Rabbit?

 It's the scary Ker-PLUNK! Hurry!

 Oh, no! A scary Ker-PLUNK! Flap, flap, flap!

 Run, run, run!

What's wrong? What's wrong?

  It's the scary Ker-PLUNK! Hurry!

 Oh, no! A scary Ker-PLUNK!
Jump, jump, jump!

 Flap, flap, flap!

 Run, run, run!

 STOP! What's wrong?

 It's the scary Ker-PLUNK!

 It's very scary!

 Very scary!

 What's a Ker-PLUNK?

 I don't know.

Just then, a big nut falls from a tree into the pond. Ker-PLUNK!

 Help! A scary Ker-PLUNK! Run, run, run!

 Silly rabbit! A big nut fell in the pond. It made the sound Ker-PLUNK.

 What? Is the Ker-PLUNK a nut?

 Yes.

 That's not scary.

 No.

 Oh, well. Let's go home.

  Goodbye, wise lion!

 Goodbye, silly animals. Good luck!

2 Characters in the story

Who are the characters in this story?

Which characters are silly?

Which character is wise?

3 Scary things

Why is Rabbit scared?

What really made the sound, Ker-PLUNK?

4 Questions

What questions do the animals ask in the story?

Write your favourite question.

5 Act it out

Act out the play in groups.

Choose which part you will play.

Words to remember

Find these words in the story:

a   the   run   help.

Writing tip

A question ends in a question mark.

6 Choose a project — What games can we play?

A Make a game for your class

Write action words on cards.

| stand up | jump | clap your hands | run |

| sit down | turn around | wave your hand | stop |

Choose a card and read the words to the class.
If you say **please** when you read the words –
Please jump – the class must do the action.
If you don't say **please** when you read the
words – **Jump** – they must not do the action.

B Make a 'Parts of the body' poster

Draw a body shape or use one that your teacher
will give you. Draw hair, eyes, nose and a mouth.
Write labels for parts of the body that you know:

nose   hand

knee   ear

foot   toes

Do you know any more?

C Make up a clapping game

Think up a clapping pattern. For example:

clap	right hands	clap	left hands	clap	right hands

Here are some other moves you can include:

both hands	knees	shoulders	head

Teach your hand-clapping game to the class.

L👀k what I can do!

- I can talk about ways to have fun.

- I can ask and answer questions: Can you ___?

Can you catch a big ball?

- I can say where things are.

- I can name parts of the body.

- I can read and write words with the short **u** sound.

c**u**p

4 Making things

1 Think about it What can we make with shapes?

35 **1 Read and listen**

What is in the poem and in the picture?

> **Party time**
> Look at me.
> What do you see?
> I can be a clown
> With a funny frown.
> Or a king
> With a silver ring.

Come to a PARTY!

36 **2 We're going to a party!**

Listen to Lucy. Her family is going to a party.
Point to Lucy. What is she wearing?

Listen, point and say.

| dress | shirt | trousers | jacket |

| skirt | shoes | glasses | hat |

Then listen to Lucy's family. Can you find them in the picture?

4 💬 Who are you?

Pretend you are going to a party!
Tell your partner who you are.
Say what you are wearing.

> I'm a pilot.
> I'm wearing a pilot's hat.

clown   princess   king   superhero   pilot   cook

5 📝 [AB] Draw and write

Draw a picture of you in your party clothes.
Write what you are wearing.

Writing tip

When we say **I am**, the words join together.
We write it like this: **I'm**.

53

2 Find out more Colourful quilts

1 Before you read

Look at the photo. This colourful
blanket is called a quilt.
Look for different shapes.
Can you see squares and triangles?
Can you see rectangles?

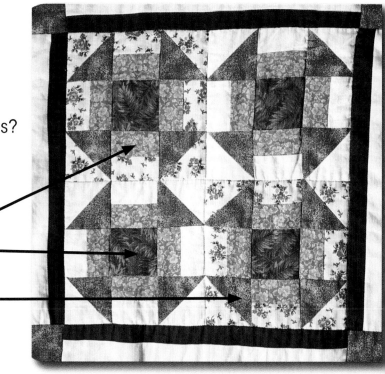

rectangle

square

triangle

38 2 Read and listen

What are the missing words?

Mei-Mei is from China.

She likes red, black and white.

She's cutting squares and circles.

Kevin is from the USA.

He likes orange, purple and __ .

He's cutting triangles and __ .

3 Paper shapes

Look at the picture.
What is the boy saying?

4 Making things with paper shapes

What are the children making? Read and find out.

The boy is making a paper quilt with his shapes.

The girl is making a picture with her shapes.

5  It's your turn!

Cut some paper shapes. Make a paper quilt or a picture with your shapes.
Talk to your partner. Ask and answer questions.

What are you doing?

I'm cutting blue squares.
I'm making a picture.

3 Letters and sounds Short e

1 Listen and look

Listen to the short **e** sound. Say the words.

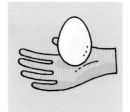

egg

pen

2 Rhyming words

Can you find the rhyming words in picture 1 and picture 2?
Make a rhyme for picture 3.

1

The hen has a pen.

2

Meg has an egg.

3

_____

3 Higgledy Piggledy

Listen to the rhyme. Say it.

Higgledy Piggledy
My black h**e**n.
She lays **e**ggs
For g**e**ntlem**e**n.
Sometimes nine and sometimes t**e**n.
Higgledy Piggledy
My black h**e**n.

4 Phonics story

Read and listen.

Listen again. How many words do you hear with the short **e** sound?

The tent

Let's make a tent.

Look! A red tent next to the bed.

Let's put the teddy in the tent.

Let's put the jet in the tent.

Let's put the ten pens in the tent.

This tent is the best!

I like this tent!

42 1 Look and listen

Liz and her friends are painting a mural. Listen and point to Liz.
Look at the sentences. Say the missing words.

1 Liz is painting a red ___ .

2 Emily is painting a gold ___ .

3 Tina ___ ___ silver stars.

4 Marcos and Rob are painting tall ___ .

5 Liz thinks the city is ___ .

2 💬 **What are they wearing?**

Look at the picture. Say what clothes
the people are wearing.

> Marcos and Rob
> are wearing ___ .

> Emily is wearing ___ .

Tina　　Liz　　Marcos　　Rob　　Emily　　the teacher

3 🎵 A traditional song

Listen to the song. Sing it with your class and do the actions.

London Bridge is falling down

London Bridge is falling down,
Falling down, falling down.
London Bridge is falling down,
My fair lady.
Build it up with **silver** and gold,
Silver and gold, **silver** and gold.
Build it up with **silver** and gold,
My fair lady.

4 🎵 Make a new song

Sing some new verses. Choose the colours you like.
Choose a building in your town – maybe your school!

We are painting London Bridge,
London Bridge, London Bridge.
We are painting London Bridge,
My fair lady.

We can paint it **red** and gold,
Red and gold, **red** and gold.
We can paint it **red** and gold,
My fair lady.

5 Read and respond

1 Before you read

This story is about elves. An elf is a magical creature in traditional stories.

As you read, think about these questions:
How do the elves help the shoemaker?
How does the shoemaker help the elves?

The elves and the shoemaker

1 The shoemaker is making shoes.

I'm very tired.

2 The shoemaker is sleeping.
The elves are making the shoes.

Let's help the shoemaker.

3

It's morning. The shoemaker wakes up.

4

The shoemaker is selling the shoes.

5

The shoemaker is very tired.
The elves are working.
The shoemaker is watching.

6

The shoemaker is selling more shoes. He wants to thank the elves.

7

The shoemaker is making a present for the elves.

8

The elves are happy.
The shoemaker is happy too.

2 Think about the story

What is the title of the story?

Who are the characters in this story?

How do the elves help the shoemaker?

How does the shoemaker help the elves?

3 Clothes in the pictures

Can you find these clothes in the pictures?

jacket   trousers   dress

shirt   hat   shoes

Language detective

Look at page 62.

Find 2 words that mean

the same as **beautiful**.

4 Puppets

Make some puppets and act out the story.

Words to remember

Find these words in the story:

is   are   look   these.

6 Choose a project What can we make with colours and shapes?

A Make a fashion model

Cut out and colour the clothes.
What is your model wearing?
Write about your fashion model.

My model is wearing black trousers and a blue jacket.

B Make a shape animal

Use triangles, circles, squares and rectangles.
Write about your shape animal.
Can your friends find the shapes?

Can you find these shapes?
2 yellow circles
2 brown triangles
2 orange triangles
2 blue circles

c Draw a picture

Draw a picture of the elves making something.
Write about your picture.

The elves are making a jet.

LOOk what I can do!

- I can talk about shapes.

- I can say what I am wearing.

- I can say what people are doing.

- I can read and write words with the short **e** sound.

egg

5 On the farm

1 Think about it What can you find on a farm?

45 1 Read and listen.

Point to the pictures of the things in the poem.

Farm poem

Hello to the farmer,
Hello to the tractor,
Hello to the cows in their stall.
Hello to the fields,
Hello to the chicks,
Hello to you all!

46 2 Interviews with farm families

A television reporter is talking to the
people on farms around the world.
Listen and find the correct picture.
Practise the conversations with
your partner.

Listen, point and say.

feeding

planting

picking

driving

carrying

Listen to the sentences. Say the missing words. Point to the matching photos on page 66.

The boys are feeding the ___ .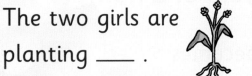

The man is driving a ___ .

The two girls are planting ___ .

The little boy is picking ___ .

4 💬 **Act it out**

Act out one of the sentences above. Can your friends guess what you are doing?

5 📝 AB **Draw and write**

Draw a picture of yourself helping on a farm. What are you doing? Write a sentence about it.

Are you planting rice?

Yes, I am.

2 Find out more   Life cycles

1 🔬 Before you read

Look at the diagram of the life cycle of a hen. Follow the arrows. Can you explain what happens?

Language detective

A life cycle goes round and round, like a bicycle wheel.
Can you find the word **cycle** in **bicycle**?

48 2 Read and listen

The life cycle of a hen

A tiny chick grows inside an egg.

The chick comes out of the egg.

The yellow chick eats and grows.

The chick becomes a hen. The hen lays an egg.

3 Animals that lay eggs

Which three animals lay eggs?

68   Unit 5 Lesson 2 Vocabulary: animals, seeds Read/Listen: life cycles

4 🗨 Before you read

Look at the diagram of the life cycle of a bean.
Explain what happens.

49 5 Read and listen

The life cycle of a bean

A seed is planted in the ground.

There are seeds inside the bean.

The seed starts to grow.

A bean grows on the plant.

The seed becomes a big plant.

6 Things that grow from seeds

Which three things grow from seeds?

(a) (b) (c) (d) (e)

7 📝 🆎 Draw and write

Write and draw the life cycle of a duck or a goose.

goose   duck

gosling

duckling

3 Letters and sounds   Short i

50 1 Listen and look

Listen to the short **i** sound. Say the words.

Add the short **i** sound to make
the name of this animal.

c h _ c k

Listen to the sound of **ch** in **chick**.
Can you think of two more words beginning with **ch**?
The pictures will help you.

50 2 Tongue twisters

A tongue twister is very difficult to say. It twists your tongue!
Say each tongue twister three times. Have fun!

Six sisters sing to six sick sheep.

How many sticks can a big chick kick?

Pick a big fig.

70   Unit 5 Lesson 3 Listen: short *i* sound Phonics: tongue twisters; *Fix-it-Fish* Talk: acting out a story

3 Phonics story

Read and listen.

Listen to the sound of **sh** in **fish**.

Listen again. Which words do you hear with the short **i** sound?

Fix-it Fish

This fish can fix things.

I can fix this ship.

He is fixing a ship.

Can you fix it?

Yes, I can.

He is fixing a swing.

Can you fix my wing, please?

Yes, I can. Just a minute.

Thank you, Fix-it Fish!

You're welcome!

He can fix tails, fins and wings.

4 Puppets

Make some puppets. Act out the story.

4 Use of English Farm activities

1 🔬 Growing vegetables

Lots of vegetables are growing on this farm.
Which vegetables are growing above the ground?
Which vegetables are growing under the ground?

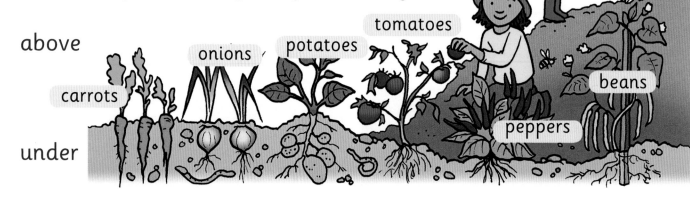

above

under

tomatoes
potatoes
onions
carrots
beans
peppers

2 💬 Ask and answer

Ask questions about the picture.
Make sure your partner gives the right answer!

Are the carrots growing under the ground?

Yes, they are.

Is the girl picking a pepper?

No, she isn't.

3 📝 AB Grow a bean plant

Grow a bean plant in a jar.
Draw a picture and label it.
Write about the bean plant.

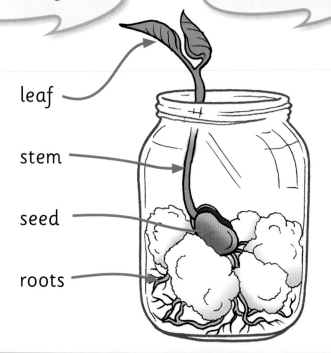

leaf

stem

seed

roots

4 🎵 Noisy animals

Listen to the animals on the farm. Which animals can you hear?
Point to the picture.

Now sing the song.
Make the animal noises!

verse 1   verse 2   verse 3

Old MacDonald had a farm

Old MacDonald had a farm, E-I-E-I-O.
And on that farm he had a cow, E-I-E-I-O.
With a moo moo here and a moo moo there
Here a moo, there a moo, everywhere a moo moo!
Old MacDonald had a farm, E-I-E-I-O.

5 📝 🎵 Sing some new verses

Draw a farm animal on a card. Put all the cards together.
Pick a card and sing that verse.

About the story

This folktale is told in many countries. It was probably first told in Russia.

53 1 Before you read

What is Little Red Hen doing?
Are the other animals helping her?

Little Red Hen

I am making bread today.

Hello, Duck.
Hello, Chick.
Can you please help me pick the wheat?

Sorry, I'm busy.

Me too.

I am picking the wheat myself.

2 Think about the story

Who are the characters in this story?

Which characters are not very helpful?

Does the story have a happy ending or a sad ending?

Why do you think this?

3 Story map Little Red Hen

Look at the story map and say what is happening.

Little Red Hen is picking the wheat.

4 🗨 Same and different

Do you know another story about Little Red Hen? How is it the same as this story? How is it different? Talk about it with your class.

5 🗨 Act it out!

Act out the story. Can you find **I'm** and **we're** in the story?

Writing tip

Some words can be joined together.

I am = **I'm**

we are = **we're**

Words to remember

Find these words in the story:

am   me   you   too.

77

6 Choose a project   What can you find on a farm?

A Make an alphabet chart

Think of things you can find on a farm.
Can you find a word for each letter of the alphabet?

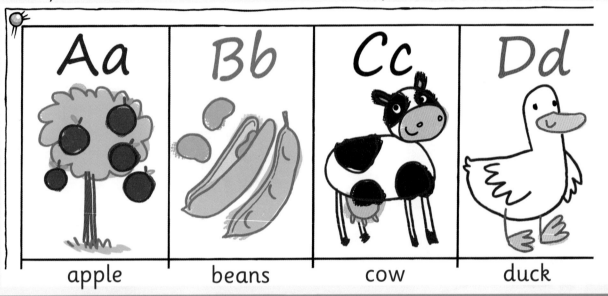

| apple | beans | cow | duck |

B Draw a map of a farm

Draw animals and plants. Write the words. Show your map to the class.
Tell the class about your farm. What are the animals doing?

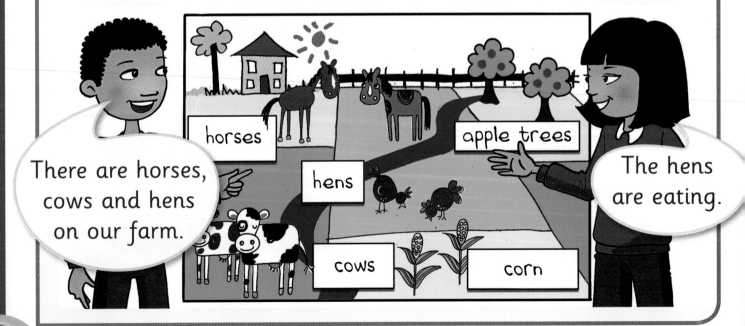

C Learn a poem

Act out the words or draw pictures.
Teach the poem to your class.

My garden

Dig a little hole. Plant a little seed.
Pour a little water. Pull a little weed.
Chase a little bug. Where did it go?
Here comes the sun! Watch my garden grow.

LOOk what I can do!

• I can name things on a farm.

• I can say what people and animals are doing.

• I can say what I am doing.

• I can read and write words with the short **i** sound.

pick fix __ __ __

79

6 My five senses

1 Think about it   How do we use our five senses?

54 **1 Read and listen**

Point to your **eyes**, **ears**, **nose** and **mouth**
as you say the words.

Two little eyes

Two little eyes to see all around.
Two little ears to hear each sound.
One little nose to smell what's sweet.
One little mouth that likes to eat.

55 **2 In the park**

Listen and point to the things in the picture.

Listen, point and say.

see   hear   smell   taste   touch

Listen to the sentences. Say the missing word.

Then look at the poem again. Which of the five senses is **not** in it?

4 💬 AB Your five senses

Look at the picture of the park.

Say what you can **see**, **hear**, **smell**, **touch** and **taste** in the park.

5 AB 🎵 Sing a song

Five musicians are playing in the park. Listen to their instruments:

1 piano **2** violin **3** bass drum **4** saxophone **5** triangle.

Sing the song. Pretend you are playing each instrument.

The music man

I am the music man. I come from down your way.

And I can play.

What can you play?

I can play the **piano**, the **piano**, the **piano**.

I can play the **piano**, **pia-piano**.

6 Guessing game

Pretend to play an instrument. Can your friends guess the instrument?

2 Find out more   Using your five senses

1 💬 Seeing

Find five things that are different in Picture A and Picture B.

Picture A

1 There are 2 girls and 1 ___ .
2 The ___ is playing the drums.
3 The ___ is a circle.
4 There are ___ drums.
5 The ___ are playing ___.

Picture B

1 There is 1___ and 2 ___ .
2 A ___ is playing guitar.
3 The ___ is a rectangle.
4 There are ___ drums.
5 The ___ are playing ___.

2 📝 💬 AB Smelling

Talk about smells!

Do you like the smell of onion?

Yes, I do.

No, I don't.

onion

fish

soap

mango

flowers

smoke

Make a list of your class's favourite smells.

Draw a picture and write a sentence. My favourite smell is ___ .

3 [AB] Touching

Imagine you're in bed. It's dark.
Your hand touches something soft.
Is it your **teddy bear** or your **book**?
We can learn a lot about an object
by touching. We can tell if it is:

soft or hard

round or flat

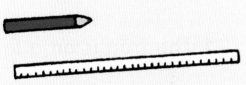

short or long

How do you think these objects feel?

ball	pencil	bat
paper clip	socks	

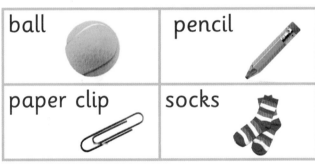

4 [💬] Touch and tell

Play this game. Can you guess what's in the bag?

How does it feel?

It feels long and hard. Is it a ruler?

No, it isn't.

Is it a pencil?

Yes, it is!

5 [💬] Hearing: Shake and listen

Play the same game with a box. Shake and listen. What's in the box?

3 Letters and sounds   Short o

58 **1 Listen and look**

Listen to the short **o** sound.
Say the words. Use the words
to make a sentence.

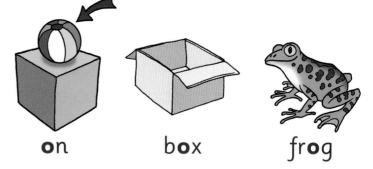

o**n**   b**o**x   fr**o**g

2 Which picture?

Match the picture to the sentence.

1 The frog is on a log.

a

2 The fox is on a rock.

b

3 The fox is hot.

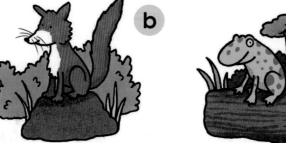

c

59 **3 Popcorn**

Listen to the rhyme. Say it. Act it out.

You put the oil in the pot,
And you let it get hot.
You put the popcorn in,
And you start to grin.
Sizzle, sizzle, sizzle, sizzle,
Pop, pop, pop!

Which words in this poem have the short **o** sound?

4 [AB] **Phonics story**

Read and listen. Which words do you hear with the short **o** sound?

Tick, tock, hop!

1

Hi. My name is Bob.

Bob, the frog, hops to the pond.
Hop, hop, stop. Hop, hop, stop.

2

Hi, Fred. What's that?

It's a clock.

Bob hears an odd sound.
Tick, tock. Tick, tock.
He sees his friend Fred, the fox.

3

I like that sound!

Fred hits a rock with two sticks.
Tap-tap, bop! Tap-tap, bop!

4

We like that sound!

The fish in the pond hear the sound. Flip, flop. Flip, flop.

5

Come on, Bob! You can hop too.

Two rabbits hear the sound.
Hop, hop, hop! Hop, hop, hop!

6

Tick, tock.
Hop, hop, hop! We can dance to the sound of the clock!

5 💬 **Act it out**

Act out the story. You can be a clock, a frog, a fox, a fish or a rabbit.

4 Use of English   Comparing things

1 Taller and faster

An elephant is **tall**.
A tree is **taller**.
A horse is **fast**.
A car is **faster**.

Can you think of something taller than a tree?

Can you think of something faster than a car?

2 Tasting and feeling

What do you think? Talk with your partner.

sweet

Which is sweeter,
jam or cake?
I think ＿＿ is sweeter.

jam

cake

cold

Which is colder,
yogurt or ice cream?
I think ＿＿ is colder.

yogurt

ice cream

juicy

Which is juicier,
an apple or
a watermelon?
I think ＿＿ is juicier.

apple

watermelon

Writing tip

When you compare things, add **-er** to the word:

cold + **-er** = **cold*er***

tall + **-er** = **tall*er***

When the word ends in **y**, the **y** changes to **i**:

juicy + **-er** = **juic*ier***

61 3 The sounds of a guitar

Listen to a guitar. It can make **loud** sounds and **quiet** sounds. It can make **high** sounds and **low** sounds.
Say if the sounds are louder or quieter, higher or lower.

4 Make a guitar

Use a small box, a rubber band, and a ruler.
Hold the rubber band with your fingers. Pluck the rubber band to make a sound.

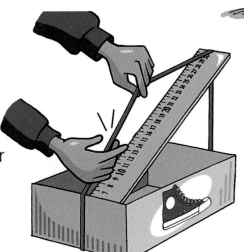

Can you make a **loud** sound? Can you make a **louder** sound?
Can you make a **quiet** sound? Can you make a **quieter** sound?
Can you make a **high** sound? Can you make a **higher** sound?
Can you make a **low** sound? Can you make a **lower** sound?

5 Make two drums

Make two different drums with two different things.
Play your drums. Which drum is louder?
Why do you think that drum is louder?

5 Read and respond

5 1 **Before you read**

2 **1 Before you read**

Listen and read to the bottom of this page. Then stop and talk.
What do you think the next friend will do and say?

About the story

This story is from India.

Five friends and the elephant

A man arrives with an elephant. It's the first elephant to visit this land! Five blind friends want to meet it. They can't see, but they can use their other senses to learn about the world.

1

The five friends go to meet the elephant.

Can we meet your elephant, please?

Of course. My elephant is tame and gentle.

2

The first friend feels the elephant's long, thin tail.

The elephant feels like a rope!

3

The second friend feels the elephant's side.

"This elephant feels like a wall!"

4

The third friend feels the elephant's leg.

"This elephant feels like a big strong tree!"

5

The fourth friend feels the elephant's ear.

"This elephant feels like a giant fan!"

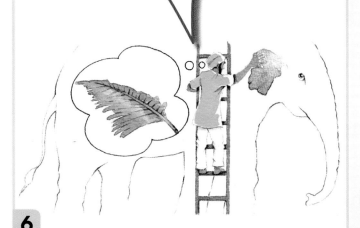

6

The fifth friend feels the elephant's trunk.

"This elephant feels like a long wiggly snake!"

7

All of you are right, my friends. My elephant has many different parts and each part feels different.

Why don't you help me take care of my elephant? You can get to know the whole elephant better.

8

The elephant smells like a horse.

The elephant has a loud voice.

The elephant likes the taste of apples.

We like this elephant!

9

So the five friends help the man take care of the elephant.
They learn many interesting things!

Words to remember

Find these words in the story:
and to friend they.

2 [AB] Parts of the elephant

Which part of the elephant feels like …

a wall?

a rope?

a snake?

a tree?

a giant fan?

ear

tail

trunk

side

leg

3 First, second, third

What happens first, second, and third in the story?

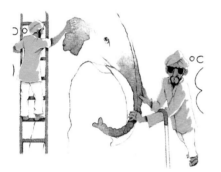

The five friends touch different parts of the elephant.

The five friends help the man take care of the elephant.

The five friends hear about the elephant. They want to meet it.

4 Special toys for all children

Here are two toys that all children can enjoy together.
How can blind children use these toys?

a ball with bells
They can ___ it.

a dice with raised dots
They can ___ it.

6 Choose a project   How do we use our five senses?

A Do a class survey

Choose a question: **Do you like this smell?** or **Do you like this sound?**
Make a survey chart.

Do you like this smell?		Ian	Dora	Sofia		
	Yes, I do.	✓				
	No, I don't.					
	Yes, I do.					
	No, I don't.	✓				

B Make a book: *My favourite things*

Write about your favourite things. Draw a picture.
Make a cover for your book.

My favourite thing to hear is the sea

page 1 My favourite thing to **see** is ____ .
page 2 My favourite thing to **hear** is ____ .
page 3 My favourite thing to **smell** is ____ .
page 4 My favourite thing to **taste** is ____ .
page 5 My favourite thing to **touch** is ____ .

C **Write a poem about a special place**

Think about a place you know. (Your bedroom, your grandma's house, the park, etc.) Use your senses as you write a poem about your special place.
Draw a picture.

Title: ____
I see ____ .
I hear ____ .
I smell ____ .
I touch ____ .

My grandpa's garden

LOOk what I can do!

- I can talk about my five senses.

- I can say how things sound and feel.

- I can compare things.

taller   colder

- I can read and write words with the short **o** sound.

fox
rock

1 Think about it   How do we travel around?

63 1 Read and listen

Where are the people from the poem?

> **Bus driver, bus driver**
>
> Bus driver, bus driver,
>
> May I have a ride?
>
> Yes, of course.
>
> Please come inside.
>
> Find a seat.
>
> Then sit down.
>
> Buckle up.
>
> We'll drive through the town.

64 2 A school trip

A teacher and some children are talking about their trip. Listen and point to the pictures.

Listen, point and say.

climb   slide   float   drive   fly

Listen to the sentences. Say the missing word.

4 Find it

Tell your partner to find something in the picture.

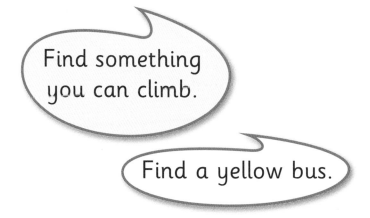

Find something you can climb.

Find a yellow bus.

Language detective

Look at the pictures above. Find a word which is something you do and also a thing.

s _ _ _ _

5 Draw and write

Draw a picture of something that you can do at the park.
Write a sentence about it.

I can ___ a ___ .

PHOTOCOPY ONLY
DO NOT CUT
OR WRITE IN BOOK

95

1 Make a helicopter

Read the instructions.

Make your helicopter.

1 Take some paper.
2 Cut out a helicopter shape.
3 Fold it.
4 Attach the paper clip.
5 Fly your helicopter.

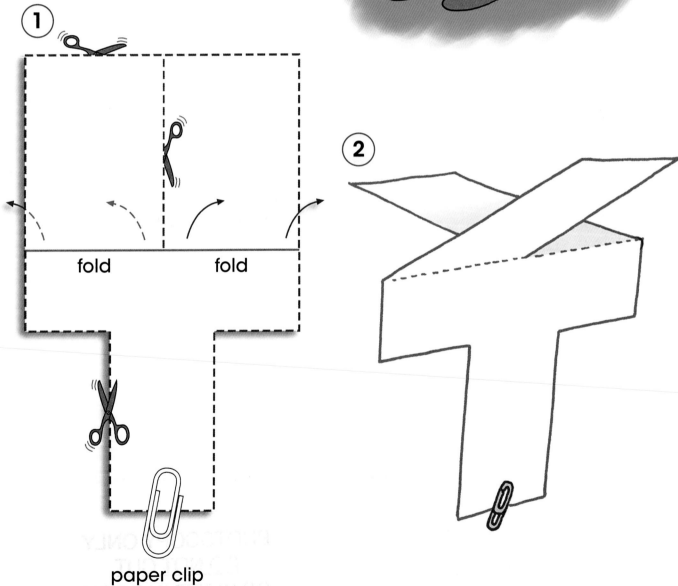

① fold   fold

paper clip

②

2 Make a plane

Read the instructions. Make your plane.

1 Choose your favourite colour paper.
2 Fold the piece of paper down the middle.
3 Fold the top corners down to the middle.
4 Bend the wings a little bit.
5 Fly your paper plane.

 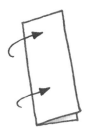  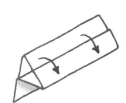 

3 💬 Helicopter race

Have a helicopter race with your partner.
Drop your helicopters at the same time.
Which helicopter stays up longer?

4 💬 Plane race

Have a plane race with your partner.
Throw your planes at the same time.
Which plane flies further?

5 📝 Write about it

Write about the races. Write the name of the winners, like this:

Marco's helicopter stayed up longer.

Ting's plane flew further.

3 Letters and sounds   Long e spelling ee

66 **1 Listen and look**

Listen to the long **e** sound.
Say the words.
Which two letters make the
long **e** sound in these words?
Which two words rhyme?

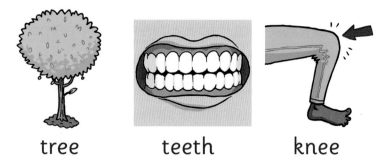

tree   teeth   knee

Add **ee** to make the name of
part of a bicycle: wh_ _l

Some question words begin with **wh**.

when   why ? ? ?

Can you think of some more question words beginning with **wh**?

2 What's in the picture?

Find things which make
a long **e** sound.

3 Questions and answers

Match the questions and answers.

1 What do bees make?

2 Where do sheep sleep?

3 What sound does a Jeep make?

a A Jeep goes BEEP BEEP.

b Bees make honey.

c Sheep sleep in a field.

4 Phonics story

Read and listen.

Listen again. Which words do you hear with the long **e** sound?

Please keep out!

5 📝 **Make a sign**

Make a 'keep out' sign. You could put it on your bedroom door!

4 Use of English   Describing things

68 1 My big blue boat

Say this poem. Do the actions.

Come for a ride in my big blue boat,
My big blue boat, my big blue boat.
Come for a ride in my big blue boat,
Out on the deep blue sea.

My big blue boat has two red sails,
Two red sails, two red sails.
My big blue boat has two red sails,
Two red sails.

2 Draw a sailing boat

You need some crayons. Tell your partner how to draw a
sailing boat. Choose colours you like.

Draw a big
green triangle.

Draw a blue line
down the middle.

Draw a long
red rectangle.

3 Describe it

Describe one of the things. Can your partner find it?

69 **4** 🎵 **The wheels on the bus**

Listen and sing. Do the actions.

The wheels on the bus
go round and round,
round and round,
round and round.
The wheels on the bus go round and round,
All day long.
The wipers on the bus go swish, swish, swish …
The money on the bus goes chink, chink, chink …
The mums on the bus go chatter, chatter, chatter …
The dads on the bus go ssh, ssh, ssh …
The bell on the bus goes ding, ding, ding …

5 📝 **Make a car park mural**

Make different coloured buses and cars. Park them in the car park.
Count them. Write some sentences about your mural.

There are 3 green buses.   There are 2 red cars.

5 Read and respond

1 Before you read

Think of some different ways to travel. How many can you think of?

70 2 Read and listen

Which of these vehicles have you travelled in?

Travelling around

There are many kinds of vehicles. They move people and things. They can go on the land, on the water and under the ground.

This is a hydrofoil. You can ride on the water in a hydrofoil. It is fast and bumpy.

This is an underground train. You can travel under the city in an underground train. It can go fast or slowly.

Some vehicles go up and down.

This is a lift. You can go up and down buildings in a lift.

This is a cable car. You can go up and down mountains in a cable car. Cable cars go slowly.

Vehicles have different numbers of wheels.

Bicycles have two wheels.

Tricycles have three wheels.

Unicycles have only one wheel.

Wheelchairs have two big wheels and two little wheels.

Some wheelchairs have three wheels. They can go very fast.

Sometimes we travel just for fun!

This is a big red skateboard. You can ride on a skateboard in the park. You can jump over things.

These people are on skis. With skis, you can go down a mountain very fast.

This is a zorb. In a zorb, you can roll down a hill very fast. You can't stop!

3 [AB] Make a chart

Look again at all the vehicles in the text.
Which ones are powered by a motor?
Which ones are powered by people?
Can you think of any more vehicles to add?

People-powered vehicles	Motor-powered vehicles
skateboard	underground train

4 My favourite vehicle

Draw a picture of a vehicle that you like.
What colour is it? Is it big or little?
Write a sentence about it.

I like my little pink plane.

Language detective

Sometimes a part of
a word helps us to
understand it.

uni = one
bi = two
tri = three
cycle = wheel

So bicycle means two wheels.
Unicycle means one wheel.
What does tricycle mean?
Can you think of another
word beginning with tri? △

6 Choose a project · How do we travel around?

A Do a travel survey

Choose 3 vehicles. Make a survey chart.

Do you like travelling by ... ?			Jack	Zhou	Bibi
bus		Yes, I do.		✓	
		No, I don't.	✓		
underground train		Yes, I do.		✓	
		No, I don't.	✓		
car		Yes, I do.	✓	✓	
		No, I don't.			

When your survey is finished, talk about your chart. How many children like travelling by bus? How many children don't like travelling by bus?

B Make a word flip book

Make a book like this.

Write these letters on the left-hand pages: **b, s, tr, kn, thr**

Write these letters on the right-hand page: **ee**

On each left-hand page, draw a picture of the word you make.

C Make up your own version of a poem

Read this poem about a plane.

Little silver plane   Over the mountains,

Up in the sky,   Over the sea,

Where are you going to   Little silver plane

Flying so high?   Please take me.

Write a poem about your favourite flying machine:

a plane   a jet   a helicopter   a kite

Is your flying machine big or little? What colour is it?
Change the words in red. Make up your own version.

Draw a picture or make a model of the flying
machine to go with your poem.

LOOk what I can do!

- I can talk about different vehicles and how they move.

- I can talk about how I move.

- I can understand simple instructions.

- I can say what colour and size something is.

- I can read and write words with the long **e** spelling **ee**. t _ _ t h

8 Wonderful water

1 Think about it Why is water important?

71 **1 Read and listen**
Then join in.

> **Rainy day**
> Rain on the green grass.
> Rain on the tree.
> Rain on the houses
> But not on me!

Today is
Monday
It is
windy and rainy

72 **2 What can you see?**

It's a rainy day. The teacher and a girl are looking out of
the window. Listen and point to the things they talk about.

3 Topic vocabulary

Listen, point and say.

  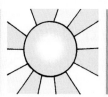 

| cloudy | windy | rainy | sunny | snowy | hot | cold |

4 💬 What's the weather like?

Look at the picture and sentence. What word is missing?
Say the whole sentence.

It is hot and __    It is cold and __

74 5 💬 Days of the week

Listen to the chant. Join in and act out the words.

Monday   Tuesday   Wednesday   Thursday   Friday   Saturday   Sunday

Ask and answer questions
with your partner.

What do you do on Tuesday?

On Tuesday, I sing a song.

6 📝 Keep a weather journal

Each day, write what the weather is like.
Draw a picture.

Today is _____. It is _____ and _____

2 Find out more | Facts about water

1 🧪 **Before you read**

What do plants need to live and grow?
What do animals need to live and grow?

75 **2 Read and listen**

We all need water

All living things need water.
Plants need water to grow.
Animals need water to drink.
People need water to drink too.

Water comes from rain and snow.
When there is no rain, the land
becomes dry and brown.

When rain comes, the land becomes
green again. Plants can grow again.
Animals and people have water to
drink again.

All living things need water.

3 Animals that live in water

Which of these animals live in water?
Make a list with your class. What other animals live in water?

frog   crocodile   hen   turtle   fish   elephant   whale

4 Write about it

Write about animals that live in water.
Choose three animals. Use the model below and fill in the missing words.
Draw a picture.

Many animals live in water.
Frogs live in water.
_____ live in water.
_____ live in water.

> **Writing tip**
>
> Remember that a sentence begins with a capital letter.
> Most sentences end with a full stop.

5 How we use water

Look at the pictures.
Read the sentences.

We use water to make soup.

We use water to wash our hands.

Think of other things we do with water.

We use water to ____ .

6 Make a class book

Make a book called **We use water in many ways**.
Write a sentence and draw a picture on each page.

76 **1 Rain poem**

Read and listen to the poem. Join in.
Look at the letters **ai** and **ay** in the words.
What sound do they make?
Find all the words with this sound.

> Rain, rain, go away.
> Come again some other day.
> All the children want to play.

2 Mystery word

Look at the sentences. Some long **a** sounds are missing.
Can you guess the missing words?
Say the sentences.
Write the words:

• Write **ai** in the middle of a word.
• Write **ay** at the end of a word.

1 It's a **r _ _ ny d _ _** .

2 Let's **p _ _ nt** a **sn _ _ l**.   **3** Let's **pl _ _** with the **tr _ _ n**.

Unit 8 Lesson 3 **Listen:** long *a* sound spellings *ai* and *ay* **Phonics:** long *a*; *Please stay and play* **Talk:** acting out a story

3 Phonics story

Read and listen. Listen again. Write the words with the long **a** sound.

Please stay and play

It's a rainy day. Little Snail is playing
with the frogs and the ducks.

'Goodbye, Little Snail' the little frogs say.
'Wait, wait! Don't go. Please stay and play.'
'Sorry, Little Snail. We need to go away.'

'Goodbye, Little Snail,' the white ducks say.
'Wait, wait! Don't go. Please stay and play.'
'Sorry, Little Snail. We need to go away.'

'Hello, Little Snail,' the big snails say.
'Hello, big snails! Please stay and play.'
'Sure, Little Snail. We can play all day.'
'Hooray!'

4 💬 **Act it out**

Who are the characters in the story? Make a list. Act out the story.

4 Use of English Things that float

1 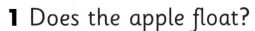 **Does it float?**

Some things float. Some things don't.
Look at the picture.

1 Does the apple float?

2 Does the paper clip float?

3 Does the pear float?

4 Does the paper boat float?

Does it float?	
Yes, it does.	No, it doesn't.
🍎	⌒

Say the sentences. Fill in the missing words.

1 The ___ floats.   **3** The ___ floats.

2 The ___ doesn't float. **4** The ___ doesn't float.

2 💬 AB **Let's find out**

You need these things:

pencil    paper   elastic band

ruler   leaf   paper clip

1 Look at each thing. Does it float? What do you think?

Does a pencil float?

Yes, I think so.

No, I don't think so.

2 Find out if you were right. Put each thing in a bowl of water.

Does it float?

78 3 🎵 Floating in a boat

Listen to the song. Look at the
picture and words.
Sing the song and do the actions.

Row, row, row your boat

Row, row, row your boat,
Gently down the stream.
Merrily, merrily, merrily, merrily,
Life is but a dream.

Row, row, row your boat,
Gently down the stream.
If you see a crocodile,
Don't forget to scream!

Row, row, row your boat,
Gently down the river.
If you see a polar bear,
Don't forget to shiver!

79 4 💬 Don't forget!

A girl and her mother are talking.
Listen. Practise the conversation
with your partner.

115

5 Read and respond

This play is from Vietnam. Some months are very dry. Farmers listen for the song of the toad. They say that it brings the rain.

80 **1 Before you read**

Here are the characters in the play.

Rooster Tiger  Bees Toad

Purple Guards Emperor Green Guards

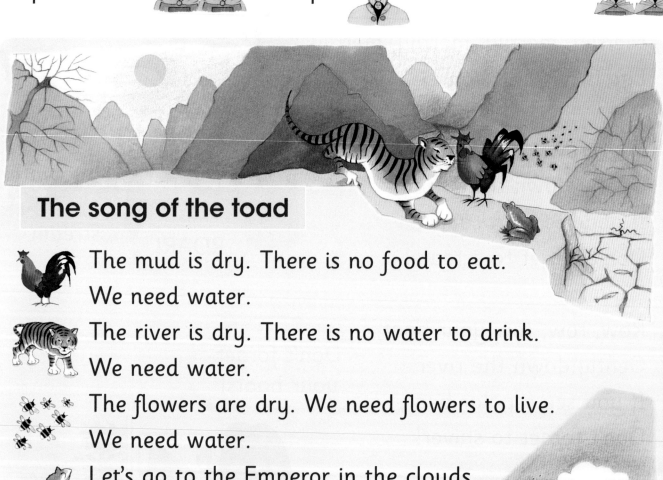

The song of the toad

The mud is dry. There is no food to eat.
We need water.

The river is dry. There is no water to drink.
We need water.

The flowers are dry. We need flowers to live.
We need water.

 Let's go to the Emperor in the clouds.
Let's ask the Emperor for rain.

Hello. I need to see the Emperor.

 No! You're a toad. A toad can't see the Emperor. Go away.

 Come, Bees! Come, Rooster! Make the Guards go away.

 Buzz, buzz.

 Cock-a-doodle-doo.

 Help! Help!

 Hello, Emperor. I need to talk to you.

 What? Green Guards, come.
There's a toad on my lap!

 Come, Tiger! Make the Guards go away.

 ROAR!

 Help! Help!

 Emperor, the earth is dry. The plants and animals need water. Please send us rain.

 OK, I can do that. I can send you rain.

It's raining!

Hooray for the rain!

Thank you, Emperor.
The next time we need rain, I will come again.

No, no! Don't come back.

Please don't come back!

Toad, you can sing when you need rain.
When I hear your song, I will send the rain.

Thank you, Emperor.

So now, when farmers hear the song of the toad, they are happy. They know that rain will come soon.

2 Characters

Look at the picture. Can you recognise all the characters?
Which characters are animals?
Why do the animals need rain?

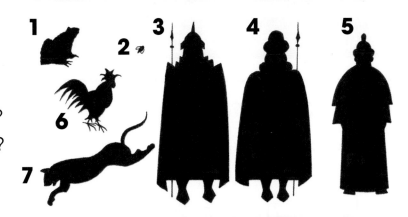

3 Play questions

Choose the right answer.

1 Where does the Emperor live?

in the clouds **on the earth**

2 What does Toad ask the Emperor to do?

to go away **to send rain**

3 Does the Emperor send the rain?

Yes, he does. **No, he doesn't.**

4 How do the animals feel when they see the rain?

scared **happy**

> **Words to remember**
>
> Find these words in the play:
> need we come no.

4 💬 Exclamation marks

You can finish a sentence with an exclamation mark. **!**
It can show that a character is scared, surprised or excited.
Look at the story. Find sentences that end with an exclamation mark.
Read them aloud to your partner. Try to sound scared, surprised or excited.

Hooray for the rain!

Help!

5 💬 Act it out

Make puppets for the animal characters.
Make hats for the Emperor and the Guards.
Act out the play.

6 Choose a project   Why is water important?

A Do a weather survey

Make a survey chart. Ask 10 children:

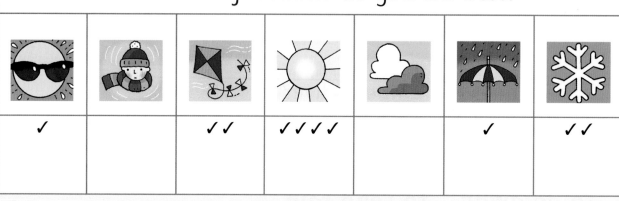

What kind of weather do you like best?						
✓		✓✓	✓✓✓✓		✓	✓✓

When your survey is finished, talk about your chart.

Which weather do most children like best?

Which weather do fewest children like best?

B Make a water world mural

Draw a big picture.

Show these things in your picture:

river   grass

mountain   flower

cloud   rain

fish   duck

toad   boat

Write the words.

Add the words to your picture.

C Do an experiment: Does your boat float?

Make a boat from paper and tape.
Put **2** coins in your boat.
Put **5** coins in your boat.
Put **10** coins in your boat.

Does your boat float?

Record the information in a table, like this.

Does your boat float?		
	Yes, it does.	No, it doesn't.
with 0 coins?	✓	
with 2 coins?	✓	
with 5 coins?		
with 10 coins?		

Make a different kind of boat. Try the same experiment. Which boat floats with more coins?

LOOk what I can do!

- I can talk about the weather.

- I can say why plants, animals and people need water.

- I can ask and answer questions about which things float.

- I can read and write words with long **a** spellings **ay** and **ai**.

r _ _ ny d_ _

9 City places

What can you see, hear and do in a city?

81 1 Read and listen

Find the traffic lights in the picture.

> **The traffic lights**
> Red means STOP.
> Green means GO.
> Yellow means WAIT,
> Even if you're late.

82 2 Walking in the city

Paco is walking home from school with his mother. Listen.
Follow his route with your finger.
Start at the school.

Listen, point and say. Listen again and clap the syllables.
How many syllables are there in each word?

city   road / pavement   shops   traffic   traffic light   bus stop

82 **4 Spot the word**

Listen again to Paco. Put up your hand when you hear
a *Topic vocabulary* word.

5 Questions

Look at the picture and answer the questions.

1 Can you find a big green bus?

2 How many **shops** are there?

3 When the **traffic light** is red,
what do the cars and buses do?

6 Play the game 'Traffic lights'

Listen to your teacher: green light is walk forward, **red** light is stop!

7  **Write and draw**

What can you **hear** in a city? What can you **see** in a city?
Make a list. Draw a picture and write sentences.

In a city, I can hear ____ I can see ____

123

2 Find out more City living

84 **1 Before you read**

Look at the photos. What can you see?
Can you find these things where
you live?

I like living in a city

I live in a city.
It's a great place to live.
There are tall buildings and short buildings.
Some buildings have gardens on top!

There's a park in my city.
It's very pretty. It has flowers,
a lake, and an ice cream seller!
I like eating ice cream in the park.

Sometimes parks and cities get dirty.
We all need to keep our city clean.
Don't forget to put your litter in a bin!

2 Over to you

Do you live in a city or in the countryside? Is there a park near you?
What other places are there where you live?

a park   a bakery   a swimming   a library   a zoo
pool

85 3 💬 Let's buy an ice cream!

Listen to the conversation. Then practise with
a partner. Choose a flavour. Choose a size.

sizes big small

86 4 🎵 Sing a city song

Listen to the song. Join in.

I live in a city

I live in a city, yes I do,
I live in a city, yes I do,
I live in a city, yes I do,
Made by human hands.

Black hands, white hands, yellow and brown,
All together built this town,
Black hands, white hands, yellow and brown,
All together makes the wheels go 'round.

by Malvina Reynolds

3 Letters and sounds   -y endings

87 **1 Listen, say and clap**

Clap the syllables of the words: **my city**.

How many syllables are there in **my**?

How many syllables are there in **city**?

2 Different sounds of -y

The words **my** and **city** both end with **-y**, but the **-y** has a different sound.

Words with 1 syllable	Words with 2 syllables (or more)
my try	city pretty
The **-y** sounds like the long **i**.	The **-y** sounds like the long **e**.

87 **3 Which -y sound?**

Say each word. Clap and count the syllables. What sound does **-y** have?

baby   cry   carry   fly   happy   rainy   sky   why

4 Which -y word?

Use one of the words above to finish each sentence.

Say the sentence to your partner.

1 It's a ___ day. Don't forget your umbrella!

2 The ___ is blue today.

3 ___ are you sad?

4 I ___ when I am sad.

5 I can ___ all my teddies.

6 Look! I can ___ !

7 I'm not sad. I'm ___ !

8 A ___ is very small.

5 Opmosites

These words are opposites:

dirty   clean   noisy   quiet

What is the opposite of **big**?

88 6 Opposites poem

Read the poem. Say the words that are missing. Then listen to check.
Match the photos with the pairs of opposites.

Opposites

The opposite of **yes** is **no**.

The opposite of **stop** is ____ .

The opposite of **good** is **bad**.

The opposite of **happy** is ____ .

The opposite of **hot** is **cold**.

The opposite of **new** is ____ .

The opposite of **wet** is **dry**.

The opposite of **hello** is ____ .

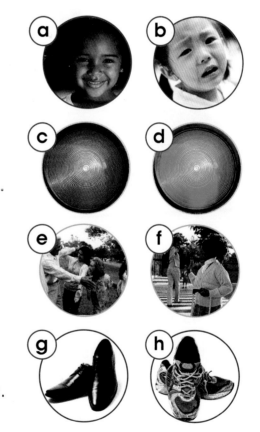

Find the words that rhyme in the poem.

38 7 Act it out

Think of actions for the words in the poem. Act it out as you listen.

127

4 Use of English   This or that?

89 **1 The Fix-it kids**

Listen to the children. They are mending some things. Point to the things that they say.

Speech bubble: **This** ball is round.

Speech bubble: **That** ball is flat.

Read the conversations. Can you fill in the missing words?
Listen again to check.

My friend and I like fixing things.

This ball is round.

____ bucket is clean.

This chair has ____ legs.

This frog is ____ .

____ teddy bear has eyes.

We are the Fix-it kids!

That ball is ____ .

That bucket is ____ .

____ chair has three legs.

That frog is ____ .

____ teddy bear doesn't have eyes.

2 **Act it out**

Act out the conversation with your partner.
Point to the objects in the picture.

3 💬 Play a game: What's this? What are these?

You need 12 counters. You need 2 players.

How to play:

1 Player 1 points to a picture and asks a question. For one thing:

What's this?

Or for more than one thing:

What are these?

2 Player 2 says the word and puts a counter on the picture.

Or player 2 says:

I don't know.

PHOTOCOPY ONLY
DO NOT CUT
OR WRITE IN

3 Play until all the pictures have a counter.

Tip: If you don't know how to say the word, look in the *Picture dictionary* at the end of this book.

4 Words I know

Which words in the game do you know well?

Which words do you need to practise more?

About the author

Lois Lenski wrote this poem.
She was an American poet.

90 1 Before you read

You are going to read a poem written in American English. Here are some words that are different in British and American English. Look out for the American words in red as you read the poem.

British English		American English
pavement	=	sidewalk
underground train	=	subway
shop	=	store
lift	=	elevator

Sing a song of people

Sing a song of people
Walking fast or slow;
People in the city,
Up and down they go.
People on the sidewalk,
People on the bus;
People passing, passing,
In back and front of us.

People on the subway
Underneath the ground;
People riding taxis
Round and round and round.

People with their hats on,
Going in the doors;
People with umbrellas
When it rains and pours.

People in tall buildings
And in stores below;
Riding elevators
Up and down they go.

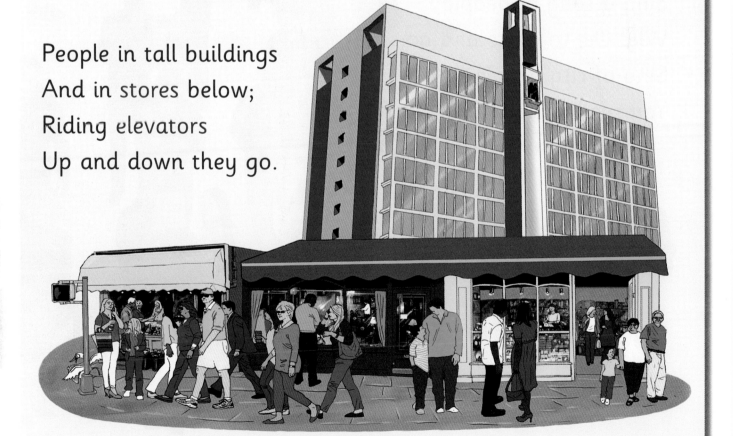

People walking singly,
People in a crowd;
People saying nothing,
People talking loud.

People laughing, smiling,
Grumpy people too;
People who just hurry
And never look at you!

Sing a song of people
Who like to come and go;
Sing of city people
You see but never know!

2 💬 Picture search

In the first picture, can you find …
- people on the sidewalk?
- people on the bus?

In the second picture, can you find …
- people on the subway?
- people in taxis?
- people with umbrellas?

In the third picture, can you find …
- people in stores?
- people in elevators?

In the fourth picture, can you find …
- people in a crowd?
- people laughing and smiling?
- grumpy people?

Where am I?

3 Where is the goose?

The goose is in every picture. Find him and say where he is.

4 💬 Perform the poem

Divide into groups. Your group will have one verse of the poem. Draw a picture for your verse. Practise saying your verse with your group. Perform the whole poem. Say your verse and show your picture.

Words to remember

Find these words in the story:
people   with   on   in.

6 Choose a project What can you see, hear and do in a city?

A Write a poem

Write a poem about your town. Think of things you can **see**, **hear**, and **smell**. Draw a picture.

My town
I can see ___ .
I can see ___ .
I can see ___ .
I can hear ___ .
I can smell ___ .
My town is ___ .

Choose an ending for the last line of your poem:

a busy place   a happy place   a noisy place   a quiet place

B Draw a city map

Make a map of a city, town or village.
Write words on your picture.

Ideas for your map:

road   pavement
park   school
shops   bus stop
bus   taxi
tall buildings
traffic lights

C Make an opposites book

Make a list of all the opposites you know.
Draw a picture or find photos for each pair of opposites.
Make a cover for your book.

up | down

L👀k what I can do!

- I can name things in a city.

- I can name opposites.

- I can talk about things using **this** and **that**.

This ball is round.   That ball is flat.

- I can read and write words that end in **-y**.

my cry city b _ _ _

baby

boy

brother

children

dad/father

family

girl

grandma

grandpa

grown-ups

mother/mum

sister

ball

book

chair

classroom

clock

computer

crayons

door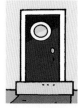

friends

map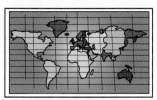

paper

pen

pencil

picture

ruler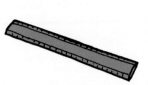

school

scissors

table

teacher

window

3 The body and clothes

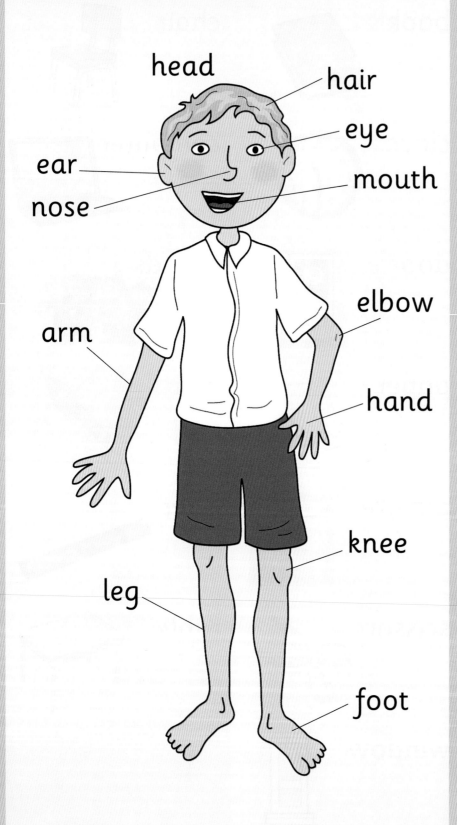

head

hair

eye

ear

mouth

nose

elbow

arm

hand

knee

leg

foot

dress

glasses

hat

jacket

trousers

shoes

shirt

skirt

4 Food

apple

banana

beans

bread

carrot

egg

grapes

ice cream

milk

noodles

onion

orange

pear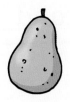

pepper

popcorn

potato

rice

soup

strawberry

watermelon

5 Actions

catch

clap

dance

draw

drink

eat

hear

jump

read

run

see

sing

sit

sleep

stand

swim

talk

throw

walk

write

6 Animals

bee

bird

cat

chick

cow

dog

duck

elephant

fish

fox

frog

hen

horse

rabbit

rooster

sheep

snail

snake

tiger

turtle

7 Nature and weather

cloud

day

flower

garden

grass

lake

leaf

night

pond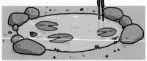

rain

river

rock

seed

sky

snow

stick

sun

tree

water

mountain

8 The city (and transport)

bike/bicycle

boat

bridge

building

bus

car

city

helicopter

house

library

park

people

plane/airplane

shop/store

street/road

subway

swimming pool

traffic lights

train

zoo

Acknowledgements

The authors and publishers would like to thank the following for their contribution to the development of Stage 1:
Series Editor: Kathryn Harper; Development Editor: Frances Reynolds; Reviewers: Paula Coudannes Landa; Liam Egan, MSc in TESOL; Lois Hopkins, MA Publishing; Ana Pérez Moreno, Licentiate in English Language and in Education; Claire Olmez, BEd, MA ELT; Mary Spratt; Graham Wilson.

Cover artwork: Bill Bolton

The authors and publishers acknowledge the following sources of copyright material and are grateful for the permissions granted. While every effort has been made, it has not always been possible to identify the sources of all the material used, or to trace all copyright holders. If any omissions are brought to our notice, we will be happy to include the appropriate acknowledgements on reprinting.

Text
pp. 18–20 adapted from *I Went to School This Morning* by Richard Brown and Kate Ruttle, 1996, © Richard Brown and Kate Ruttle, illustrations © Margaret Chamberlain, published by Cambridge University Press, adapted and reproduced with permission.

p. 124 Lyrics of 'I Live in a City' words and music by Malvina Reynolds. Copyright 1960 Schroder Music Co. (ASCAP). Renewed 1988. Used by permission. All rights reserved.

pp. 130–132 'Sing a Song of People' by Lois Lenski, Covey Foundation Inc., reprinted by permission of SLL/Sterling Lord Literistic, Inc. Copyright by Lois Lenski.

Other songs and music throughout are reproduced from *Primary Music Box* © Cambridge University Press

Photographs
p.12 *1* Chris Stowers / Panos Pictures; p.12 *2* Gallo Images / Getty Images; p.12 *3* wavebreakmedia / Shutterstock; p.13 *tl* Paul Rushton / Alamy; p.13 *tr* Imaginechina/Corbis; p.13 *bl* Angela Hampton Picture Library / Alamy; p.13 *bc* DAYLIGHT/Balan Madhavan / Alamy; p.13 *br* Still Pictures / Robert Harding Pictures; p.21 *l-r* plherrera / iStockphoto; p.21 jcrader / iStockphoto; p.21 36clicks / iStockphoto; p.21 jabejon / iStockphoto; p.22 track5 / iStockphoto; p.26 *1* kali9 / iStockphoto; p.26 r Still Pictures / Robert Harding Pictures; p.27 aldomurillo / iStockphoto; p.32 *1* spectrelabs / iStockphoto; p.32 *2* Still Pictures / Robert Harding Pictures; p.32 *3* Panorama Productions Inc. / Alamy; p.32 *4* Monkey Business / Thinkstock; p.33 *5* sjlocke / iStockphoto; p.33 *6* Hutchings Stock Photography/CORBIS; p.33 *7* Jupiterimages / Thinkstock; p.33 *8* digitalskillet / iStockphoto; p.34 *9* Alaska Stock / Alamy; p.34 *10* Still Pictures / Robert Harding Pictures; p.54 DougMcPhoto / iStockphoto; p.66 *a* iStockphotos / Thinkstock; p.66 *b* Ashley Cooper / Robert Harding; p.66 *c* baona / iStockphoto; p.66 *d* Jaggat Rashidi / Shutterstock; p.66 *e* Harry Hook / Getty Images; p.68 clockwise from the top NREY / Shutterstock, Ljupco / iStockphoto, Tsekhmister / iStockphoto, IvonneW / iStockphoto; p.70 Ljupco / iStockphoto; p.79 *l* Ashley Cooper / Robert Harding; p.79 *r* iStockphotos / Thinkstock; p.82 *tl* Nattika / Shutterstock; p.82 *tc* criben / Shutterstock; p.82 *tr* Marjan Veljanoski / Shutterstock; p.82 *bl* kaband / Shutterstock; p.82 *bc* Narongsak / Shutterstock; p.82 *br* onyxproduction / iStockphoto; p.83 *tl* darklord_71 / iStockphoto; p.83 *tc* t_kimura / iStockphoto; p.83 *tr* pappamaart / iStockphoto; p.83 *bl* slobo / iStockphoto;

p.83 *br* Africa Studio / Shutterstock; p.86 Jam Africa Studio / Shutterstock; p.86 Cake Picsfive / Shutterstock; p.86 Yoghurt Marc Dietrich / Shutterstock; p.86 Ice Cream vm / iStockphoto; p.86 Apple Cameramannz / iStockphoto; p.86 Watermelon ozgurdonmaz / iStockphoto; p.91 *l* Layne Kennedy/CORBIS; p.91 *r* Le-Dung Ly/ Science Faction/Corbis; p.92 *t* kaband / Shutterstock; p.92 *b* criben / Shutterstock; p.93 Ice Cream vm / iStockphoto; p.93 Yoghurt Marc Dietrich / Shutterstock; p.98 Erdosain / iStockphoto; p.100 Sirimo / iStockphoto; p.102 *l* Rhombur / iStockphoto; p.102 *r* McKevin / iStockphoto; p.103 *tl* vm / iStockphoto; p.103 *tr* tma1 / iStockphoto; p.103 *cl* greenland / Shutterstock; p.103 *cc* EML / Shutterstock; p.103 *cr* Ramona Heim / Shutterstock; p.103 *bl* Blend Images / Alamy; p.103 *br* Daniel Korzeniewski / Shutterstock; p.104 Mike McGill/CORBIS; p.104 gorillaimages / Shutterstock; p.104 Imgorthand / iStockphoto; p.107 Vivian Fung / Shutterstock; p.109 *l* bluehill75 / iStockphoto; p.109 *r* sianc / Shutterstock; p.110 *t-b* Robert Churchill / iStockphoto, iStockphoto / Thinkstock, hadynyah / iStockphoto, Jason York / iStockphoto; p.111 *l* kataijudit / Shutterstock; p.111 *r* hxdbzxy / Shutterstock; p.121 hxdbzxy / Shutterstock; p.124 *t-b* Andrey Yurlov / Shutterstock, stocknshares / iStockphoto, KirbusEdvard / iStockphoto, Peter Alvey / Alamy; p.127 *a* Studio1One / iStockphoto; p.127 *b* zhangyang13576997233 / Shutterstock; p.127 *c* jallfree / iStockphoto; p.127 *d* jallfree / iStockphoto; p.127 *e* Blend Images / SuperStock ; p.127 *f* Superstudio / Getty images; p.127 *g* Oleksii_Sagitov / iStockphoto; p.127 *h* wakila / iStockphoto; p.129 *1* malerapaso / iStockphoto; p.129 *2* temniy / iStockphoto; p.129 *3* simonkr / iStockphoto; p.129 *4* esolla / iStockphoto; p.129 *5* Eric Isselee / Shutterstock; p.129 *6* Archipoch / Shutterstock; p.129 *7* Agorohov / Shutterstock; p.129 *8* Anna Omelchenko / Shutterstock; p.129 *9* IlexImage / iStockphoto; p.129 *10* Maica / iStockphoto; p.129 *11* alexsl / iStockphoto; p.129 *12* pagadesign / iStockphoto; p.133 Pressmaster / Shutterstock; p.134 *t* AJP / Shutterstock.com; p.134 *b* Peter Phipp/Travelshots.com / Alamy

Key: *t* = top, *c* = centre, *b* = bottom, *l* = left, *r* = right.

Development of this publication has made use of the Cambridge English Corpus (CEC). The CEC is a multi-billion word computer database of contemporary spoken and written English. It includes British English, American English and other varieties of English. It also includes the Cambridge Learner Corpus, developed in collaboration with Cambridge English Language Assessment. Cambridge University Press has built up the CEC to provide evidence about language use that helps to produce better language teaching materials.

This product is informed by the English Vocabulary Profile, built as part of English Profile, a collaborative programme designed to enhance the learning, teaching and assessment of English worldwide. Its main funding partners are Cambridge University Press and Cambridge English Language Assessment and its aim is to create a 'profile' for English linked to the Common European Framework of Reference for Languages (CEFR). English Profile outcomes, such as the English Vocabulary Profile, will provide detailed information about the language that learners can be expected to demonstrate at each CEFR level, offering a clear benchmark for learners' proficiency. For more information, please visit www.englishprofile.org